Practical Chinese Reader II
Patterns and Exercises

Simplified Character Edition

实用汉语课本

Practical Chinese Reader II
Patterns and Exercises

Simplified Character Edition

汉字作业簿

简体字本

陈 凌 霞
Ling-hsia Yeh

Cheng & Tsui Company
Boston, Massachusetts

About the Author: Ling-hsia Yeh is assistant professor of Chinese in the Department of Asian Languages and Literatures, University of Massachusetts, Amherst. She received her B.A. degree in Foreign Languages and Literatures from National Taiwan University, and the M.A. and Ph.D. degrees in linguistics from Indiana University.

Cheng & Tsui Company, Inc.
25 West Street
Boston, Massachusetts 02111

Simplified Character Edition: ISBN: 0-88727-160-X
Traditional Character Edition: ISBN: 0-88727-161-8

Printed in the United States of America

PUBLISHER'S NOTE

The Cheng & Tsui Company is pleased to announce the most recent volume of its Asian Language Series, *Practical Chinese Reader II: Patterns and Exercises*. This workbook supplements the highly successful introductory Chinese language textbook *Practical Chinese Reader II*, compiled by the Beijing Language Institute.

The Beijing Language Institute is the leading institution teaching Chinese as a foreign language in the People's Republic of China and produces many significant and valuable language texts. Unfortunately, many of these texts have not been widely known or available in the West. The C & T Asian Language Series is designed to publish and widely distribute important Beijing Language Institute texts as they are completed in China, as well as other significant works in the field of Asian languages.

We welcome readers' comments and suggestions concerning the publications in this series. Please contact the following members of the Editorial Board:

Professor Shou-hsin Teng, Chief Editor
Dept of Asian Languages and Literature
University of Massachusetts, Amherst, MA 01003

Professor Samuel Cheung
Dept of Oriental Languages, University of California, Berkeley, CA 94720

Professor Ying-che Li
Dept of East Asian Languages, University of Hawaii, Honolulu, HI 96822

Professor Timothy Light
President, Middlebury College, Middlebury, VT 05753

Professor Stanley R. Munro
Dept of East Asian Languages and Literature
University of Alberta, Edmonton, Alberta, Canada

Professor Ronald Walton
Dept of Hebrew and East Asian Languages and Literature
University of Maryland, CollegePark, MD 20742

PREFACE

This workbook was written with the intention of providing a companion to the textbook **Practical Chinese Reader, Book II,** compiled by the Beijing Language Institute. Although it is meant to be a sequel to **Practical Chinese Reader I: Patterns and Exercises** by Professor Madeline Chu of Kalamazoo College, Michigan, it does not follow entirely the format and approach adopted in her book.

The organization of the workbook is such that for each lesson, except review lessons, there is a grammar review followed by a set of exercises. The grammar review attempts to provide an overall presentation of the grammar and sentence patterns in every lesson. A certain portion of the exercises are designed to reflect those patterns and their usages. The students are then required to decide what to use and when to use their knowledge of the grammar in the related exercises. The grammar notes follow as closely as possible the explanations in the textbook with the exception of lessons 39 and 47, where certain verb-type words are considered as post-verbal prepositions rather than resultative verb complements.

The goal of the exercises is to familiarize students with the vocabulary, sentence structure, and content of every lesson. There are generally four to five exercises in each lesson. The forms frequently employed include fill-in blanks, word-order, answer questions, complete sentences, structural change, and translation. The arrangement of the exercises for each lesson is such that practice on vocabulary comes first, followed by those on structure and content, with the translation exercises at the very end since they require knowledge of both vocabulary and grammar.

Not many compositional exercises are included since they can always be assigned by individual instructors to serve their own needs. The compositional exercises given in this workbook are controlled ones in the sense that vocabulary and sentence structure for writing the compositions are controlled within the limit of related lessons. At the same time, students are still allowed to stretch their imagination.

A few words must be said about some of the English sentences in the translation exercises. Although they may not sound idiomatic, those sentences are written deliberately either to correspond to the structures of their Chinese counterparts or to give clues to certain Chinese structures. This is done to avoid the possibility of coming up with misleading translations for the exercises.

The author welcomes comments and suggestions from users of this volume. This author alone is responsible for any mistakes that may be found in this book.

Ling-hsia Yeh
University of Massachusetts, Amherst
January, 1991

ACKNOWLEDGMENTS

I am grateful to the Five Colleges East Asian Languages Program for providing me with a grant which made possible the completion of this work in its present form.

I should like to express my sincere appreciation to the following people for their assistance and encouragement:

Members of the Editorial Board of the Cheng & Tsui Company's *Asian Language Series* for their comments and suggestions for revising the manuscript;

Professor Donald Gjertson for going over the translation exercises and for polishing the sentences;

Professor Shou-hsin Teng for his encouragement and generous loan of the Chinese computer software program used in producing this work;

Ms. Jiaxiang Dai for typing the translation exercises.

I should like to express special thanks to Mr. Tong Shen, a Ph.D. candidate in the linguistics department of the University of Massachusetts, Amherst, for typing, editing, and printing the manuscript numerous times. Without his patience and meticulous work, the final draft would not have been completed in its present form.

Finally, I would like to thank my colleagues, and especially Nina Rose-Racine, of the Department of Asian Languages and Literatures for their moral support.

Ling-hsia Yeh
University of Massachusetts, Amherst

ABBREVIATIONS

Adjective	Adj
Adverb	Adv
Aspect	Asp
Interrogative Pronoun	IP
Negation	Neg
Noun Phrase	NP
Object	Obj
Other Element	OE
Preposition	Prep
Question Device	QD
Subject	Subj
Stative Verb	SV
Verb Phrase	VP

Note: Words with asterisk following them are those given in the supplementary vocabulary lists.

CONTENTS

Interaction between time-measure complements (TMC) and verbal -了 as well as the sentential 了

I. Regular pattern

   A. Verbs without objects

      1. Habitual or future events

         Subj (+ OE) + Verb + TMC
         他   每天   学习   两个小时。
         (He studies for two hours every day.)

      2. Past events

         Subj (+ OE) + Verb + -le + TMC
         他   昨天   锻炼   了   一个小时。
         (He exercised for an hour yesterday.)

         王老师 在中国   住   了   三个月。
         (Professor Wang stayed in China for three months.)

      3. Events which took place in the past and have been carried into the moment of utterance

         Subj (+ OE) + verb + -le + TMC + le
         我   已经   学习   了   两个小时 了。
         (I have been studying for two hours.)

   B. Verbs with objects

      1. Habitual or future events

         Subj (+ OE) + Verb + Obj + Verb + TMC
         他   想   学习   汉语   学习   一年。
         (He intends to study Chinese for a year.)

      2. Past events

         Subj (+ OE) + Verb + Obj + Verb + -le + TMC
         他   在中国   学习   汉语   学习   了   一年。
         (He studied Chinese in China for a year.)

      3. Events which took place in the past and continued to the moment of utterance

         Subj (+ OE) + Verb + Obj (+ OE) + Verb + -le + TMC + le
         他   在中国   学习 汉语 已经   学习   了   一年   了。
         (He has been studying Chinese in China for a year.)

1

II. Insertion pattern

This pattern applies to sentences with non-specific verbal objects and only if the objects are not pronouns.

Subj (+ OE) + Verb + (-le) + TMC + (de) + Obj + (le)
他   想   学习   两年   的   汉语。
(He intends to study Chinese for two years.)

他   昨天   看   了 一个小时 的   电视。
(He watched television for an hour yesterday.)

我   已经   坐   了 十个小时 的   飞机   了。
(I have been on the airplane for ten hours.)

III. The usage of 多 with a numeral

A. When the numeral is 'ten' or less

Numeral + Measure + 多 + Noun
  三   个   多   小时

B. When the numeral is 'ten' or more

Numeral + 多 + Measure + Noun
  三十   多   个   小时

C. Exceptions: 天 and 年 behave like measure words.

三年多
四天多
三十多年
二十多天

2

Fill in appropriate vocabulary:

1. 你在这儿住了多长 ____ ____ 了?

2. 你学了 ____ 年中文了?

3. 1965年我 ____ 二次回中国,参观了很多工厂。

4. 北京是中国的 ____ ____ 。

5. 一天有二十四个 ____ ____。

6. 去中国以前我们先要去办 ____ ____ 。

7. 北京的机场是一个 ____ ____ 机场。

8. 中国是一个 ____ ____ 主义的国家。

9. 中国希望 ____ ____ 四个现代化。

10. 我的妈妈很 ____ ____ ,每天工作十个小时。

11. 在外国住了很久的中国人叫 ____ ____ ____ 。

12. 希望你们能 ____ 国家作一点事。

13. 我在上海住了三 ____ 多月。

Word order:

1. 我　　回国　　1963年　　第一次

2. 我　　住了　　在　　三个多月　　上海

3. 你家里　　在北京　　有人　　还　　吗

4. 我　　三十　　教书　　已经　　多　　了　　年　　教了

5. 学生代表　　是　　北京　　的　　语言学院　　我

6. 坐　　飞机　　你们　　多长　　了　　时间　　的

7. 不错　　北京　　真　　天气　　的

8. 我弟弟　　两年　　准备　　学习　　在中国　　多

9. 有　　中文系　　老师　　位　　十　　多

10. 到北京　　十分钟　　有　　还　　要　　就　　了

Complete the following sentences with phrases containing time-measure complements.

1. 我们三点钟到国际机场，现在六点半，朋友还没来，我们等他已经

    _____.

2. 他九点十分去买东西，九点五十五分开车回家．他 _____

    的东西．

3. 我的朋友今年夏天要去中国学习汉语，他想明年冬天回美国． 他

    准备在中国 _____.

4. 昨天我们早上十点坐飞机，中午十二点半到那个大城．我们 ____

    _____.

5. 我们每天上午十点十分上汉语课，十一点五分下课． 我们每天

    _____汉语课．

6. 1965年王老师开始在外语学院教书． 他现在已经 _____

    _____.

7. 我每天晚上十一点睡觉，早上七点起床． 我每天 _____

    _____.

8. 那些代表们晚上七点开始开会*，现在九点四十分． 他们 ____

    _____.

Translate into Chinese (using regular pattern):

1. How many hours do you work every day?

2. He lived in the capital for half a year.

3. I hope I will be able to stay in China for three months.

4. How long did that overseas Chinese visit that factory?
   More than two hours.

5. That student representative has been waiting for him for
   twenty minutes.

6. How many months has he lived in the countryside?
   More than four months.

7. They did not watch TV for the whole evening. They only
   watched for a half hour or so.

8. Are you going to use the car for a long time?
   I will use it for three days.

9. Prof. Wang has been teaching in that college for over
   thirty years.

10. I have been on the plane for more than ten hours.

I. Translate into Chinese (using insertion pattern):

   1. How long have you been riding on the train?

   2. They watched movies for two hours and forty minutes.

   3. The students have been holding a meeting for the whole evening.

   4. Twenty some teachers shopped for one and a half hours yesterday.

   5. This overseas Chinese intends to study Chinese for one year and a half.

II. Translate the following dialog:

A: Haven't seen you for a long time. Where have you been?
B: I went to China for three months.
A: Was it the first time that you went to China?
B: No, it was the second time.
A: Is there anyone in your family who lives in China?
B: Yes, my older brother.

I.   The experiential aspect marker 过

> Subj (+ Neg/OE) + Verb + Asp +   NP   (+ QD)
> 我   最近   看   过   那个电影。
> (I saw that movie recently.)
>
> 我   没(有)   看   过   那个电影。
> (I have never seen that movie.)
>
> 你   看   过   那个电影   吗/没有?
> (Have you ever seen that movie?)

II. Verb-过 and frequency

A.   An expression of frequency follows a verb and its aspect marker.

> Subj (+ OE) + Verb + Asp + Frequency
> 我   去年   透视   过   两次。
> (I had X-ray examination twice last year.)

B.   Insertion pattern is more frequently used when a verb is followed by a general noun (i.e., a non-specific noun).

> Subj + Verb + Asp + Frequency + Obj
> 我   看   过   两次   中国电影。
> (I have seen Chinese movies twice.)

C.   When the object of a verb is a pronoun or an expression of location, insertion pattern is not allowed.

> 我去过他家一次。
> (I have been to his home once.)
>
> 我弟弟见过他两次。
> (My younger brother has seen him twice.)

D.   When the object of a verb is a definite noun, it is always topicalized (i.e., placed at the beginning of a sentence) and frequency therefore follows the verb.

> 那个电影我看过两遍。
> (I have seen that movie twice.)

I. Fill in blanks with appropriate vocabulary.

1. 我去大学 ____ ____ ____ 看病。

2. 我的心脏不太好，请给我 ____ 一下血压吧！

3. 你第一 ____ 来中国吗？ 不，我 ____ 二次来．

4. 我们去医务所 ____ ____ 身体．

5. 我没 ____ 过什么大病． 七岁的时候，得 ____ 一 ____ 肺炎．

6. 检查身体以前，请先到那儿拿一 ____ 表．

7. 那个中国电影，他已经看过两 ____ 了．

8. 他最近去过两 ____ 北海．

9. 那个足球队赢过三 ____，也输 ____ 三次．

10. 这个汉字，我写过两遍了，我要 ____ 写一 ____．

11. 有人说 "有志者事竟成"． 我以前也听过 ____ ____ 的话。

12. 爸爸妈妈给我们 ____ ____。 老师给我们 ____ ____ 。

II. Identification.

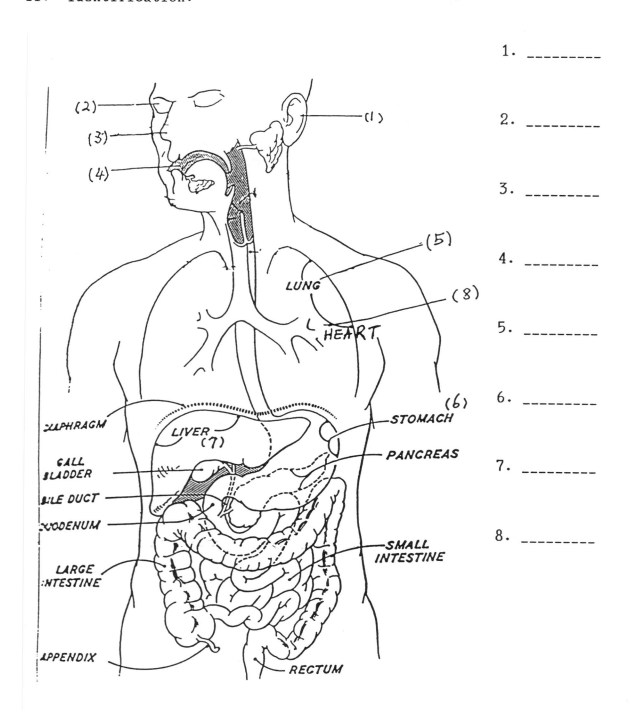

1. _____

2. _____

3. _____

4. _____

5. _____

6. _____

7. _____

8. _____

Practical Chinese Reader #32 Exercise B

Fill in blanks with 了, 过 or 0 (=nothing).

1. 这个练习，我已经看 ____ 一遍 ____，不会有错.

2. 你以前用 ____ 筷子吗?　我没用 ____.

3. 我们七点吃饭，他来 ____ 没有?　他还没来 ____ 呢.

4. 这件衬衫太小 ____，我不想买.

5. 他们来 ____ 北京一个多星期 ____，参观 ____ 很多地方.

6. 对 ____，我十岁的时候去 ____ 英国，在那儿住 ____ 三个月.

7. 你会用 ____ 毛笔写 ____ 中文吗?

8. 他看电视已经看 ____ 两个小时 ____.

9. 那本书我已经念 ____ 两遍 ____.

10. 我昨天没复习 ____ 课文，我忘 ____ 今天有汉语课.

11. 他来 ____ 找 ____ 你三次.

12. 我们就要 ____ 去 ____ 中国访问.

11

Word order:

1. 血压　　一下　　去　　他　　　量　　　医务所

2. 电视里　　中国电影　　　几次　　我　　　在　　　看过

3. 心脏　　血压　　和　　我的　　正常　　都　　　吗

4. 透视　　到　　请　　一下　　对面房间　　　吧

5. 还　我　　一遍　　这个电影　　　看　　　想

6. 可以　　以后　　透视　　就　　了　　　走

7. 希望　要　　我　　自己　　锻炼　　注意

8. 小时候　　病了　　得过　　我　　两个月　肺炎

9. 拿　你　　去　一张表　　内科　　再　　先在那儿
   量　血压

10. 哪些地方　　来北京　　星期　　了　你们　　过　　一个
    去　多

12

Practical Chinese Reader #32 Exercise D

Translate into Chinese:

1. Have you seen this movie before?
   No, I have never seen it.

2. My father has had a physical check-up recently.

3. Have you ever had a serious illness?
   I had pneumonia when I was ten years old.

4. How many times have you had your blood pressure measured?

5. Have you ever seen a doctor at that infirmary?
   Yes, I have seen doctors there three times.

6. Last year his mother had an X-ray examination once.

7. I have listened to this song several times. I would like
   to listen to it once more.

8. How many times have you read that (literature) book?

9. How many times have you been to that place?
   I have been there four times.

10. Please take a look at this form.

11. We asked them to tell us about Beijing for a while.

12. I have never heard such saying before.

13. Before you see the doctor, go to the internal medicine
    department first to get a form.

I. Sentential particle 了 which occurs at the end of a sentence
    may indicate a change of state.

   A. Sentences with stative verbs (or adjectival predicates)

        Subj   (+ OE) +   SV   +   le
        天气   冷   了。
        (It is getting cold.)

        树上的叶子 都   红   了。
        (All the leaves have turned red.)

        雨   小   了.
        (The rain is letting up.)

   B. Sentences with nouns as their predicates

        现在十点了，我们回家吧。
        (It is ten o'clock.   Let's go home.)

        这个孩子今年十二岁了。
        (The kid is twelve years old now.)

   C. Sentences   with   meteorological verbs   which   are   always
       subjectless

        下雨了。   (It is raining.)

        刮风了。   (It is windy.)

   D. Sentences with 'verb to be', 'verb to have', modals, and
       non-adjectival type stative verbs

        现在他是大学生了。   (He is a college student now.)

        他有工作了。   (He has a job now.)

        我会说汉语了。   (I can speak Chinese now.)

II. The construction 不...了 also indicates a change of state.
     It implies that a circumstance no longer exists.

        不下雪了。   (The snow has stopped.)

14

Fill in blanks with appropriate vocabulary.

1. 有人 ＿＿＿＿ 门，请你去开门，好吗?

2. 春天来 ＿＿＿＿，花园里的花都 ＿＿＿＿ 得很好.

3. 这儿的冬天很冷，时间也很长，常常 ＿＿＿＿ 风，＿＿＿＿ 雪.

4. 秋天的时候，树上的 ＿＿＿＿ ＿＿＿＿ 都红 ＿＿＿＿，大家都喜欢去看红叶.

5. 张老师教我们一 ＿＿＿＿ 古诗.

6. 梅花不 ＿＿＿＿ 冷，也不怕雪. 文学家 ＿＿＿＿ 梅花写 ＿＿＿＿ 不少诗.

7. 天气预报* ＿＿＿＿ 明天会下雪.

8. A. 北京的天气 ＿＿＿＿ ＿＿＿＿ ＿＿＿＿ ?

   B: 不错.

9. 那儿的夏天天气很热，最热的时候到过一百 ＿＿＿＿.*

10. 五分钟以前还下雨，现在雨 ＿＿＿＿ 了.

11. 今天冷吗? 我不 ＿＿＿＿ ＿＿＿＿ 很冷，我觉得很暖和.

12. 那儿的天气很好，天天 ＿＿＿＿ 是晴天.

Word order:

1. 公园　玩儿　今天　很好　你们　吗　天气　没到

2. 有人　我　很热　夏天　告诉　北京的　以前

3. 秋天　是　树上的　了　红　叶子　现在　都　了

4. 梅花　大风　天气　大雪　很好　开　的　得　在

5. 今天　到　写　梅花　文学家　为　不少　了　从
　　诗　古时候

6. 冬天　在　有　花　什么　中国

7. 晴天　下雨　现在　今天上午　了　是

8. 常常　冬天　北京的　刮风　下雪

9. 不早　我们　时间　以后　谈　了　吧　再

10. 那本书　你　的　要　这是

Complete the following sentences:

1. 下雪的时候，这儿很漂亮．你应该 _____．

2. 这儿的夏天很热，我以前不习惯，现在 _____．

3. A：他告诉我他要去检查身体．

   B：不，他有事儿，他 _____．

4. 现在是春天了． _____．

5. 秋天到了， _____．

6. 冬天来了， _____．

7. 我以前很喜欢喝咖啡，现在 _____．

8. A：你再坐一会儿．

   B：不， _____．

9. 雨停了， _____．

10. 我弟弟以前不会游泳， _____．

Practical Chinese Reader #33 Exercise D

Translate into Chinese:

1. What time is it (now)?
   It is nine o'clock now. We shall set off pretty soon.

2. It is spring (now). All the flowers are in blossom.

3. It was raining when I came this morning. It is snowing (now).

4. It is summer (now). The weather is getting hotter.

5. Has the rain stopped?
   No, it is still very heavy.

6. He told me that he was going to have a physical check-up today.
   No, he is busy. He will not go.

7. My younger brother is a college student (now). He can drive (now).

8. I liked swimming when I was young, but I do not like it any more.

Practical Chinese Reader #33 Exercise E

Translate into Chinese:

1. We watched football game on TV from 2:30 till 4:45.

2. A: Is it far from here to his house?

   B: Not far. It only takes ten minutes to get there.

3. A: Someone told me that winter in Beijing is long. The
      lowest temperature ever is ten degrees centigrade
      below zero.

   B: That's right. I think that spring in Beijing is best.
      The weather is really nice. It is neither cold nor
      hot. It is sunny everyday.

   A: I heard that the Summer Palace is beautiful in summer.

   B: But it is even more beautiful when there is snow.

Practical Chinese Reader #33 Exercise F

Write a paragraph describing your reading of the cartoon.

20

The aspect marker 着 indicates a continued state. Possible cases employing the aspect are as follows.

A.   An action verb followed by 着

>   Subj   (+ Neg) + Verb + Asp (+ NP)   (+ QD)
>   他   拿   着   一封信。
>   (He is holding a letter.)

>   那个女孩子   穿   着   一件红衬衫   吗/没有?
>   (Does that girl wear a red blouse?)

>   营业员   没   看   着   书。
>   (The clerk was not reading a book.)

B.   The state of an inanimate subject

>   房间里的灯没开着。
>   (The light in the room was not on.)

>   学校的门开着没有?
>   (Is the gate of the school open?

C.   When a locative expression is the focus of a sentence

>   Location (+ Neg) + Verb + -zhe + NP   (+ QD)
>   墙上   挂   着   一张图片。
>   (A picture was hung on the wall.)

>   牌子上   没   写   着   汉字。
>   (Chinese characters were not written on the sign.)

>   柜台上   放   着   邮票   没有?
>   (Were stamps placed on the counter?)

D.   Structures with serial verbs where 着 is attached to the first verb to form a verbal phrase describing the manner in which the second verb is performed.

>   Subj (+ OE) + Verb1 + Asp (+ NP1) + Verb2 (+ NP2)
>   他们   站   着   写   信。
>   (They stood while writing letters.)

>   我   喜欢   喝   着   咖啡   听   音乐。
>   (I like to drink coffee while listening to music.)

21

Fill in blanks with appropriate vocabulary.

1. 这个房间的窗户前边 ＿＿＿＿ 着一张床。 床上 ＿＿＿＿ 着一本书。床下 ＿＿＿＿ 着一双鞋。墙上 ＿＿＿＿ 着一张画儿。画上 ＿＿＿＿ 着梅花。 旁边还 ＿＿＿＿ 着一首诗。

2. 外边有两个人，都 ＿＿＿＿ 着大衣。两人手里都 ＿＿＿＿ 着帽子。

3. 包裹里边装* ＿＿＿＿ 一 ＿＿＿＿ 帽子和两 ＿＿＿＿ 衬衫。

4. 他热情 ＿＿＿＿ 说："我会认真 ＿＿＿＿ 学习。"

5. 王老师笑 ＿＿＿＿ 对我说："我很高兴你能到中国去学习。"

6. 我不知道这 ＿＿＿＿ 信是谁寄的。 信封上没写 ＿＿＿＿ 寄信人的姓名。

7. 我去他家的时候，他正打 ＿＿＿＿ 电话呢!

8. 公园里边有很多人，有的坐 ＿＿＿＿ 说话，＿＿＿＿ ＿＿＿＿ 玩着球。

9. 在邮局、商店里工作的人我们叫他们 ＿＿＿＿ ＿＿＿＿ ＿＿＿＿。

10. 我想很快 ＿＿＿＿ 告诉他这个新闻，我不知道我应该 ＿＿＿＿ 信还是 ＿＿＿＿ 电报。

11. 我到邮局去 ＿＿＿＿ 一封信。

12. 营业员给我七 ＿＿＿＿ 邮票，二十 ＿＿＿＿ 信封。

Word order:

1. 一个　牌子　牌子　挂着　写着　前边　上边　窗口　字

2. 邮局里　营业员　大声　的　地　问　你　买　什么　要

3. 要　邮局　航空信　给　朋友　去　我　寄

4. 明信片　邮票　和　柜台　放　里边　很多　着

5. 姓名　地址　你的　和　下边　写　要　还

6. 医务所　一张　拿　他　表　去　检查　着　身体

7. 食堂里　有的　吃饭　人很多　坐着　站着　有的　买菜

8. 上课的时候　注意地　他　学习　下课的时候　认真地　他　听

9. 很多电影　有的　有的　喜欢　不喜欢　看过　我　我　我

10. 图片　字　写着　没　为什么　字

Answer the following questions:

1. 你的房间住着几个人？

2. 你喜欢坐着看书还是站着看书？

3. 寄英文信的时候，寄信人的姓名和地址在信封上边还是在信封下边？

4. 在中国寄中文信的时候，收信人的地址在信封上边还是在信封下边？

5. 寄航空信快还是寄平信快？

6. 本市的邮局每天开几个小时？

7. 每天上课的时候来得晚的人，以后应该怎么样？

8. 你打过中文电报* 没有？

9. 从这儿到你家的信要多少天？

10. 你为什么学习汉语？

Translate into Chinese:

1. The clerk wore a new shirt. He was holding a postcard in his hand.

2. Was the TV in the living-room on?
   No, it wasn't on.

3. A table was placed in front of the window.

4. Many beautiful stamps were placed inside the counter.

5. A plate was hung on the wall.

6. Is the door of the post office open?
   Yes, it is open.

7. I like to drink coffee while I listen to music.

8. He answered with a smile: "The sender's name and address have to be written at the bottom."

9. He said while pointing to the chart: "You should write the envelope this way."

10. There are many people in the post office. Some are waiting to buy stamps. Some are sitting and writing letters.

Translate into Chinese:

1. While in class, the students listened attentively.

2. He said loudly to me: "Let's go swimming."

3. Do you know why this year's winter is so long?

4. I still do not know how to write some of these words.

5. Some people like to see movies; some like to listen to music.

6. My friend has many stamps. Some are Chinese ones; some are foreign ones.

7. A: Excuse me, how long does it take to send a letter to China?
   B: Regular mail or air mail?
   A: Air mail.
   B: It takes a week.
   A: I want to have it registered too.

Fill in blanks with 着，了，在 or 过.

1. 行李上没有写 ____ 他的名字.

2. 现在梅花正开 ____ 呢.

3. 我还没用 ____ 筷子吃中国菜.

4. 五月十五日就要考试 ____，考试以后就放暑假 ____.

5. 他以前当 ____ 老师，现在不当 ____.

6. 他笑 ____ 说："我在这儿已经住 ____ 两年 ____."

7. 这个字我们学 ____，可是我又忘 ____.

8. 我弟弟穿 ____ 冰鞋正 ____ 滑冰呢.

9. 你在这儿照相 ____ 没有?

10. 你在那个食堂吃 ____ 饭没有?

11. 我昨天去看他的时候，他 ____ 看电视呢.

Fill in blanks with 再，又，还 or 就.

1.　放了假，我 ＿＿＿＿ 坐飞机回家了.

2.　今年寒假我工作了一个月，挣了一些钱. 我想利用暑假 ＿＿＿＿ 挣点钱.

3.　上星期我的表停了，后来好了. 今天我的表 ＿＿＿＿ 停了.

4.　我们今天考试了，明天 ＿＿＿＿ 要考呢.

5.　我们吃饭以后 ＿＿＿＿ 谈吧.

6.　外边 ＿＿＿＿ 下雨呢!

7.　那个电影我看过两次. 我想 ＿＿＿＿ 看一次.

8.　快十二点了，他 ＿＿＿＿ 不想睡.

9.　这一次考试，我考得不好. 我想 ＿＿＿＿ 复习一下这一课.

10.　我现在不给家里写信. 我想放假了 ＿＿＿＿ 写.

11.　雨已经停了，我们 ＿＿＿＿ 要回去了.

Answer the following questions:

1. 你的专业是什么?

2. 这学期你给家里写过几次信?

3. 要口语进步应该怎么样?

4. 你说中国话的机会多不多?

5. 你们什么时候放暑假?

6. 今年暑假你想作什么?

7. 你们下学期几月开学?

8. 你了解中国的情况吗?

9. 你们多长时间考一次试?

10. 你学习了汉语以后想作什么?

Translate into Chinese:

1. They took an examination on the fourth day after arriving in Beijing.

2. Some of the students did well in the examination; some did a bit worse.

3. I feel that my speaking skill is not very good. I want to practice listening and speaking more.

4. He made great progress. He can talk with his friends in English now.

5. I was afraid that my parents would be worried. I have written them twice.

6. He used to work in the post office, but he doesn't work there any more.

7. It's December now. We are about to have the winter break.

8. He has been sick for three days. His mother is worried.

9. The doctor carefully checked his heart and said with a smile: "Your heart is normal."

10. I intend to study Chinese for a year here, then I will go to China.

Practical Chinese Reader #36 Grammar Notes

I. Comparative structures with the preposition 比

A. Comparison is made between two objects with regard to a certain quality which is expressed by a stative verb or a verbal phrase.

> Subj1 + bi + Subj2 + SV/VP
> 他　　比　我　　忙。
> (He is busier than I am.)
>
> 我　　　比　我朋友　了解中国。
> (I have better understanding of China than my friend does.)

B. Structures with adverbials of degree
    (b's are possible but less frequent.)

1. a. Subj1 + Verb + de + bi + Subj2 + SV
        他　　跑　　得　比　我　　　快。
        (He runs faster than I do.)

    b. Subj1 + bi + Subj2 + Verb + de + SV
        他　　比　我　　跑　　得　　快。
        (He runs faster than I do.)

2. a. Subj1 + Verb + Obj + Verb + de + bi + Subj2 + SV
        他　　作　菜　作　　得　比　我　　　好。
        (He cooks better than I do.)

    b. Subj1 + Verb + Obj + bi + Subj2 + Verb + de + SV
        他　　作　菜　比　我　　作　　得　好。
        (He cooks better than I do.)

Note: The negative form 不比 is rarely used out of context. It is often used to negate an assertion.

Eg.　X:　我想他跑得比你快。
        (I think he runs faster than you do.)

     Y:　不，他跑得不比我快。
        (No, he doesn't run faster than I do.)

31

II. Comparative structures with 有/没有

The negative form is used more frequently while the positive form is only used in context.

A.   Subj1 + meiyou + Subj2 + SV/VP
       这间房间   没有   那间房间   大。
       (This room is not as big as that one.)

       我   没有   他   喜欢音乐。
       (I don't like music as much as he does.)

B. Structures modified by adverbials of degree
    (b's are possible but less frequent.)

   1. a. Subj1 + Verb + de + meiyou + Subj2 + SV
           他   跑   得   没有   我   快。
           (He doesn't run as fast as I do.)

       b. Subj1 + meiyou + Subj2 + Verb + de + SV
           他   没有   我   跑   得   快。
           (He doesn't run as fast as I do.)

   2. a. Subj1 + Verb + Obj + meiyou + Subj2 + Verb + de + SV
           我   作   菜   没有   他   作   得   好。
           (I don't cook as well as he does.)

       b. Subj1 + meiyou + Subj2 + Verb + Obj + Verb + de + SV
           我   没有   他   作   菜   作   得   好。
           (I don't cook as well as he does.)

32

I. Give appropriate measure words.

1. 一 ____ 茶具

2. 四 ____ 茶壶

3. 两 ____ 茶碗

4. 这个工厂不生产这 ____ 瓷器.

5. $5.96 = 五 ____ 九 ____ 六 ____

6. 一 ____ 画儿

II. Fill in blanks.

1. 这套茶具比那 ____ 便宜.

2. 这种纸没有那 ____ 薄.

3. 他游泳比我 ____ 得快.

4. 百货大楼的东西比这家商店 ____ 多.

5. 我弟弟画画儿画 ____ 没有我好.

6. 这个茶碗不 ____ 那个高.

7. 你的自行车 ____ 他的高吗? 我的没有他的高.

8. 这种冰鞋一 ____ 多少钱?

9. 这种明信片多少钱一套? 一块三 ____ 六.

10. ____ 比这套便宜的吗? 没有,这套最便宜.

Rewrite the following sentences by using the worde given in parentheses.

1. 昨天很冷．今天更冷．（比）

2. 这个售货员二十三岁．那个售货员三十岁．（比）

3. 这种瓷器薄．那种瓷器更薄．（不比）

4. 唐山生产瓷器的历史很长．景德镇生产瓷器的历史更长．（没有）

5. 这种自行车的质量好．那种自行车的质量也好．（有）

6. 他每天六点起床．我每天七点起床．（没有）

7. 他复习了五课课文．我复习了三课课文．（比）

8. 我弟弟写字写得好．我妹妹写字也写得好．（有）

9. 他进步得快．我进步得慢．（不比）

10. 我喜欢看电视．我朋友更喜欢看电视．（没有）

Word order:

1. 瓷器　玉　白　纸　薄　那儿的　比　比

2. 质量　提高了　以前　这种茶具　比　的

3. 我的　没有　他的　历史知识　多

4. 两个　我　茶壶　要　的　五元

5. 这种表　那种　便宜　有　吗

6. 很长　景德镇　瓷器　的　历史　生产

7. 六个茶碗　二毛八　一共　这套　四十二块

8. 漂亮　比　这套明信片　有　的　吗

9. 比　他　开车　我　开得　好

10. 我　她　喜欢音乐　　没有

Translate into Chinese:

1. This bicycle is cheaper than that one.

2. This kind of jade is not as thin as that kind.

3. Is the quality of this kind of china better than the quality of that kind?

4. Is this tea set as good as that one?

5. Is there anyone in your class who is younger than you are?

6. The painting on this tea pot is prettier than the painting on that one.

7. Things in the Department Store are more expensive than those in this shop.

8. Is England's history longer than China's?

9. My friend studies harder than I do.

10. This college football team does not play as well as that one.

Translate into Chinese:

1. He sings better than I do.

2. My younger sister does not read as many history books as I
   do.

3. This sales clerk speaks English better than that one.

4. This factory manufactures more tea cups than that one.

5. I do not paint as well as he does.

6. The teachers did not come as early as the students did.

7. A: How much are the postcards per set?
   B: $3.95 per set.
   A: I want two sets. How much are they altogether?
   B: $7.50 for two sets.
   A: Here is a ten dollar bill.
   B: Here is your change, $2.50.

I.   Comparative structures expressing equivalence

  A. Subj1   +   gen + Subj2 (+ bu) + yiyang (+ SV)
    这种布　　　　跟　　那种布　　　　　　一样。
    (This kind of material is the same as that kind of
    material.)

    今年的天气　跟　　去年　　　不　　一样。
    (This year's weather is different from last year's.)

    他　　　　　跟　我　　　　　　　一样　　　忙。
    (He is as busy as I am.)

  B. Subj1 + Verb + Obj + Verb + de + gen + Subj2 + yiyang (+ SV)
    他　　　说　　汉语　说　　得　　跟　　中国人　一样。
    (He speaks Chinese like a native speaker.)

    他　　　说　　汉语　说　　得　　跟　　中国人　一样　　好。
    (He speaks Chinese as well as a native speaker does.)

II.   Comparative structures with complements of quantity which
    can be non-specific as 一点儿 ('a little'),   得多 ('much
    more'), 一些 ('a little'), or specific.

    Subj1 + bi + Subj2 + SV + quantity
    今天　　比　昨天　冷　　　一点儿。
    (Today is a bit colder than yesterday.)

    这种布　比　　那种布　好看　　一些。
    (This kind of material is a little prettier than that kind.)

    他弟弟　比　他　　　年轻　得多。
    (His brother is much younger than he is.)

    这种笔　比　　那种　　便宜　五块钱。
    (This kind of pen is five dollars cheaper than that kind.)

III. A difference in quantity or time from what was originally planned or expected may be expressed by the adverbs 多, 少, 早, 晚 occurring before verbs and quantity.

我多花了十块钱。
(I spent ten dollars more.)

他少买了一张电影票。
(He bought one less movie ticket.)

我只比你早来了五分钟。
(I came only five minutes earlier than you did.)

你先走吧，我要晚走一刻钟。
(You go first. I'll leave fifteen minutes later.)

Fill in blanks with appropriate vocabulary.

1. 这件中山装跟那件 ____ ____ 肥，可是不 ____ ____ 长．那件比 这件长五公分．

2. 我的棉袄的 ____ ____ 跟你的不一样．我的是蓝的，你的是灰的．

3. 这件衣服的 ____ ____ 合适吗？ 不 ____ ____，太短了一些．

4. 这件外衣比那件长 ____ ____? 这件比那件长三公分．

5. 这种绸子多少钱一 ____? 三块八一米．

6. 这辆自行车跟那 ____ 一样新吗？ 不，那 ____ 旧一点儿．

7. 这件雨衣长70公分，那件长72公分． 这件比那件 ____ 两公分．

8. 他的表现在是一点五分，我的表是一点十分．我的表比他的 ____ 五分钟．

9. 他花了二十块钱，我花了二十五块． 他比我 ____ 花了五块钱．

10. 这种茶具十五块一套， 那种三十块一套． 这种茶具比那种 ____ ____ 得多．

11. 这双布鞋合适吗？ 小 ____ ____． 再试试这双．

12. 他吃一个面包，我吃两个面包． 我比他多吃 ____ ____．

13. 他哥哥二十岁，他十八岁． 他比他哥哥小 ____ ____ ．

Word order:

1. 七十多块　　我朋友　钱　　我　花　比　多　了

2. 三天　只　多　比　平信　寄　　寄　　　航空信

3. 中山装　　　蓝色　穿　　我　　的　有　　吗

4. 钱　我　哪儿　应该　交　　在

5. 便宜　比　布面的　绸面的　　二十块　钱

6. 好　多　　我　他　得　游得　游泳　比

7. 瘦　比　　我妹妹　我　　一点儿

8. 肥　跟　这件　那件　衣服　不一样

9. 两瓶　请　多　酒　太　了　买　少

10. 中文　一年　比　好　他　我　学了　说得
　　 可是　只　他

Answer the following questions:

1. 你穿多大号的衣服？

2. 你穿几号鞋？

3. 你有多高？

4. 你穿的外衣是中式的，还是西式的？

5. 你喜欢什么颜色？

6. 你爸爸比你妈妈大吗？ 大几岁？

7. 这儿的天气跟你家那儿一样不一样？ 哪儿比较暖和？

8. 你有绸面的中式棉袄吗？

9. 你说汉语说得跟中国人一样吗？

10. 你家的车是什么颜色的？

Translate into Chinese:

1. The color of this cotton tunic suit is the same as that one.

2. The length of this cotton-padded jacket is not the same as the black one.

3. Is the weather here same as the weather in your country?

4. This jacket fits as well as that one.

5. Does he ride a bicycle as fast as you do?

6. Did you spend as much money as he did?

7. This sales clerk speaks English like an Englishman.

8. How much is this kind of fabric per meter?

9. These Western-style suits are $119 per set.

10. The bicycles are $89 each.

Translate into Chinese:

1. This Chinese style cotton-padded jacket is a little bit shorter than that one.

2. The blue sweater is much more loose-fitting than the red one.

3. This kind of silk fabric is five dollars more expensive than that kind.

4. The custom-made table is five centimeters higher than the one you bought.

5. The kind of material I bought is a bit thicker than the kind he bought.

6. This time I paid ten dollars less than last time.

7. My friend spent twenty dollars more than I did.

8. Last month, this factory manufactured one hundred bicycles more than before.

I. Resultative verbs are normally made of two verbs. The first element indicates an action and the second element describes the result or outcome of the first verb. The second verb always has a fixed meaning. Following are some examples.

1. 好: in a good state; properly -- 放好 (to put properly); 作好 (to do something well); 记好 (to remember well)

2. 错: wrong; by mistake -- 说错 (to say something wrong); 听错 (did not hear the correct message); 看错 (did not see correctly)

3. 对: correctly -- 作对 (to do the right thing); 说对 (to say something correctly); 拿对 (to get the right thing)

4. 懂: to understand -- 听懂 (to listen and understand); 看懂 (to understand through reading or seeing);

5. 见: to perceive -- 看见 (to see); 听见 (to hear)

6. 会: to acquire a skill -- 学会 (to master)

Since a resultative verb always describes the result of an action, i.e., it refers to a completed or expected to be completed event. imperfective aspect marker 着 therefore never cooccurs with it. 了 is the most likely aspect marker to be employed.

Subj (+ Neg) + Verb + Comp (+ Asp) + NP (+ le) (+ QD)
他   看   懂   了   这封信。
(He read and understood this letter.)

我   没   看   见   他。
(I did not see him.)

他   学   会   开汽车 了   没有?
(Has he learned how to drive a car yet?)

II. Expressions of direction

往 + Direction + Verb

往   前   走。   (Go straight ahead.)

往   右   拐。   (Turn to the right.)

Fill in blanks with appropriate vocabulary.

1. 请问，到语言学院 ____ ____ 走?

2. 从这儿 ____ 南走，到红绿灯再 ____ 右拐.

3. 买两张 ____ 平安里的票.

4. 我要坐开 ____ 北海公园的车.

5. 换13 ____ 公共汽车，在哪儿下车?

6. 这路车的终点 ____ 是平安里.

7. 钢铁学院 ____ 这儿远不远?

8. 这个字很容易，你 ____ ____ 没写对?

9. 请问这是什么 ____ ____ ?　 这是东边.

10. 上课以前请先 ____ 队.

Fill in blanks with appropriate resultative complements:

1. 下飞机的人请带 ＿＿＿＿ 自己的行李．

2. 今天上午的考试不难，老师的问题我都回答 ＿＿＿＿ 了．

3. 我学中文学了快一年了，我能看 ＿＿＿＿ 容易的中文书．

4. 今天我不能开车，我的汽车还没修 ＿＿＿＿ 呢！

5. 有人敲门，你听 ＿＿＿＿ 了没有？

6. 昨天你在学校看 ＿＿＿＿ 了我哥哥没有？

7. 他说汉语说得不清楚，我没有听 ＿＿＿＿．

8. 去中国以前，你要先到中国大使馆去办 ＿＿＿＿ 签证．

9. 收信人的地址不对，你写 ＿＿＿＿ 了．

10. 我还没学 ＿＿＿＿ 开车，所以我不能开车送你去车站．

11. 我们写 ＿＿＿＿ 练习以后再去看电影吧！

12. 这路车不去百货大搂，你坐 ＿＿＿＿ 了．

13. 这个成语故事你听 ＿＿＿＿ 了没有？

Translate into Chinese (using resultative verb complements):

1. The bus is about to start. Please be seated properly.

2. I did not hear correctly the address he gave me.

3. Did you do the exercises correctly?

4. The clerk did not understand (through reading) the characters on the sign.

5. Have you seen the jacket I am looking for?

6. The worker has repaired his bicycle.

7. Sorry I'm late. I took the wrong bus.

8. This question is pretty easy. How come he didn't answer it correctly?

9. How come he didn't understand (by listening) the ticket-seller's questions?

10. I haven't learned how to use chopsticks.

Translate into Chinese:

1. A: Excuse me, how do I get to the department store?
   B: Go south from here. Make a left turn when you get to the traffic lights.

2. A: Where is the street-car station?
   B: Go west. Make a right turn at the intersection.

3. A: Two tickets for the Language Institute.
   B: You've taken the wrong bus. The direction is not right. You should take the bus which goes east.
   A: What number bus should I take?
   B: You get off at the park and transfer to number 113 bus.

4. A: How many more stops are there before the terminus?
   B: There are three more stops. Please take your things with you when getting off.

5. A: Does this bus go to the Beijing Iron and Steel Engineering Institute?
   B: Yes. Please line up to get on the bus.

Gubo （古波） went to see his friend yesterday. Write a short paragraph describing how he got to his friend's house in accordance with the given chart.

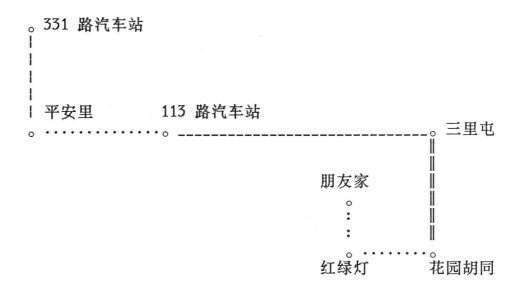

_____ 坐公共汽车

• • • • • • • • 走路

======= 坐电车

I. More resultative verbs!

1. 到 -- to succeed in
    找到 (to find); 收到 (to receive); 见到 (to see);
    拿到 (to get)

2. 完 -- to finish
    唱完 (to finish singing); 用完 (to finish using)

3. 住 -- in a fixed or proper state
    记住 (to remember well)

II. Post-verbal prepositions

Post-verbal prepositions are certain verb type words which
occur immediately after the main verb in a sentence. These
verbs should not be considered as resultative complements,
because they are more closely related to the noun phrases
following them than to the preceding verbs. They may
indicate a location or a recipient. Thus they behave more
like pre-verbal prepositions or coverbs such as 从，在，到，
把，or 用.

1. 在 -- at, on, in
    放在 (to put in/on/at); 写在 (to write ... on);
    挂在 (to hang on)

2. 到 -- to
    走到 (to walk to); 学到(第三十课) (to study to lesson 30)

3. 往 -- toward
    开往 (to drive toward)

III. Fronting of definite noun phrases

When a verb with a definite noun phrase as its object is
followed by the post-verbal preposition 在, the object is
fronted to the beginning of the sentence in which it occurs.
For example:

那套明信片我放在桌子上了。
(I placed the set of postcards on the table.)

今天的练习我写在纸上。
(I wrote today's exercises on the paper.)

IV. Sentence connectives

A. The construction 一 ... 就 ('as soon as') functions as a
connective associating two sentences. Both 一 and 就 must
precede a verb. If the subjects of the two sentences are
identical, the second one may be deleted.

Subj1 + yi + Predicate1 (+ Subj2) + jiu + Predicate2
我   一   放假   就   回国。
(I will return to my country as soon as the vacation
 begins.)

他   一   教   大家   就   会了。
(Once he started teaching, everyone learned.)

B. 虽然 ... 但是/可是 -- although ... but

虽然他没来过中国，可是对北京了解得很多。
(Although he has never been to China, he knows a lot about
 Beijing.)

他虽然没来过中国，但是对北京了解得很多。
(Although he has never been to China, he knows a lot about
 Beijing.)

52

I. Fill in blanks with proper verbs and resultative complements.

1. 上午我去宿舍找他，可是没 _____ 他.

2. 上个月我阿姨说要从中国给我来信，我昨天 _____ 她的信了.

3. 我可以用你的词典吗?

   可以，但是 _____ 了请放在我的书桌上.

4. 我妈妈到百货大楼去买那种茶具，可是没 _____，因为他们没有那种茶具.

5. 我在哪儿办手续? 在那儿. _____ 了手续请到对面透视.

6. 老师讲的语法，我记了，可是没 _____，都忘了.

7. 今天下午大学队和工人队赛球. _____ 了以后，大家一起去吃饭.

II. Fill in blanks with proper main verbs and post-verbal prepositions.

1. 我的帽子在哪儿? 你的帽子 _____ 墙上呢!

2. 他的名字，我 _____ 本子上了.

3. 昨天晚上我作练习 _____ 十二点钟.

4. 这学期我们学了很多课汉语. 我们现在 _____ 第三十九课了.

5. 你要的那本书我没带来，我 _____ 家里了.

6. 请问，到邮局怎么走? 你 _____ 红绿灯以后，往右拐.

7. 我的外衣，你放好了吗? 我 _____ 箱子里了.

Word order:

1. 邻居　我们　很关心　对　我们的

2. 的　意思　吗　成语　懂　你　这句

3. 了　天气　是　虽然　春天　还是　现在　很冷　已经　但是

4. 弟弟　的　是　权叔　爸爸

5. 在街上　能　他　可是　作一些工作　虽然　退休　还　已经
   了　他

6. 愉快的　我们　记住　一天　这个　永远　要

7. 笑　小姑娘　了　客人　就　看见　一　这个

8. 吃饭　留　客人　下来　请　远方的

9. 选举　上月　车间主任　当了　他　车间里

Answer the following questions according to the content of the
text in this lesson.

1. 古波和帕兰卡上星期去丁云家，他们见到了丁云家里的什么人？

2. 丁云她爸爸作什么工作？

3. 丁云的妈妈现在怎么样？

4. 帕兰卡为什么说丁云家的邻居也非常热情？

5. 小兰是谁？　她今年几岁？

6. 丁云爸爸怎么说他自己？　那句话是什么意思？

7. 丁云妈妈留古波和帕兰卡吃饭，他们留下来了没有？　为什么？

8. 那一天古波和帕兰卡过得很愉快．对那一天，他们要怎么样？

Practical Chinese Reader #39 Exercise D

Translate into Chinese:

1. A: Listen! Someone is knocking at the door.
    B: I didn't hear it.

2. A: Did you receive letters from your uncle?
    B: No. But I received a letter from my aunt this morning.

3. A: Have they finished studying this book?
    B: Not yet.

4. This student did not memorize the vocabulary well.

5. I've looked for my notebook all morning, but I didn't find it.

6. Have you received the bicycle he gave you (as present)?

7. It was pretty late when I walked to the station.

8. We have already studied up to lesson thirty.

Translate into Chinese:

1. I put the notebook you bought on the table.

2. Where did you write your neighbor's address?

3. The guests left as soon as we finished eating. Nobody stayed.

4. As soon as he heard this piece of news, he cried.

5. As soon as the retired teacher returned to his home, he saw his younger sister running to the street to welcome him.

6. Although he is smart, he does not understand the meaning of this sentence.

7. Although he said that he would remember that day forever, he soon forgot it all.

Fill in blanks with sentence particles 呢，吧，or 了.

1. 现在是夏天 ____，天气已经很热 ____.

2. A：今年秋天你要回国 ____？

   B：不，我不回国，我还要在中国住半年 ____.

3. A：我们在哪儿下车 ____？

   B：我们在终点站下车 ____.

4. A：别看电视 ____，现在已经七点 ____，电影快开始 ____.

   B：你先走 ____，我不想去看电影 ____.

5. A：昨天晚上他们在家作什么 ____？

   B：我去的时候他们正看电视 ____.

6. A：他们已经拿到表 ____，你们 ____？

   B：我们也拿到 ____.

7. A：再吃点 ____.

   B：谢谢，我已经吃得很多 ____.

8. 我们还没见过面 ____. 你是学生代表王小蓝 ____？

9. 运动会就要开始 ____. 观众都站在操场旁边，可是主席还没到
   主席台上 ____.

10. A：这次的百米赛他一定能打破记录，你 ____？

    B：不，我能保持记录就很好 ____.

Fill in blanks with resultative complements.

1. 有人敲门，你听 ____ 了没有?

2. 他激动地说："网球赛已经打 ____ 了，我输了."

3. 观众们鼓 ____ 了掌以后，主席开始说话了.

4. 他跑到百米的终点那儿的时候看 ____ 了很多观众站在那儿.

5. 你听 ____ 广播了吗? 没有，太远了，我没听 ____.

6. 那个运动员跑得快极了，他打 ____ 了男子百米赛的记录.

7. 这是谁的表? 别拿 ____ 了.

8. 这一课的生词你都记 ____ 了吗?

9. 他找 ____ 了他的照片了没有?

10. 我每天洗 ____ 澡以后才吃早饭.

11. 今天早上他去接他的叔叔，接 ____ 了没有?

Practical Chinese Reader #40 Exercise C

Answer the following questions:

1. 你喜欢什么运动?

2. 夏天最好的运动是什么?

3. 你参加过运动会吗?

4. 你会不会打太极拳?

5. 看运动比赛的时候你激动吗?

6. 你有没有你爸爸高?

7. 今天是不是比昨天冷?

8. 你说汉语说得跟你的老师一样好吗?

9. 你常常听新闻广播吗?

10. 作完这个练习以后你要作什么?

60

Practical Chinese Reader #40 Exercise D

Translate into Chinese:

1. The audience applauded warmly for the athletes.

2. He does not play Taijiquan.

3. Who got the highest score in this examination?

4. He was very excited during each ball game, but I was even more excited than he was.

5. There are so many people coming to attend the sports meet.

6. This athlete is only 0.1 second faster than the other one.

7. Nobody broke the record in the men's one hundred meter race. Xiao Zhang kept his own record of 11.2 seconds.

8. The athletic field at our school is much bigger than the one at their school.

9. Who is the fastest runner in this sports meet?

10. The tea set she bought is the same as the tea set you bought, but hers was cheaper than yours.

I. Verbs with directional complements: A full-fledged verbal phrase with a directional complement comprises three verbs -- V1 V2 V3. V1 normally indicates action; V2 indecates position; V3 expresses direction (toward or away from the speaker). Following are examples of the verbs which may fall into different groups.

> V1: 拿，带，跑，走，寄，送，买，找，请
>
> V2: 进(in)，出(out)，上(up)，下(down)，回(back)，过(over)
>
> V3: 来，去

There are possible combinations of these verbs.

> A. V2V3: 进来，出去，上来，下去，进去，回去，过来，etc.
>
> B. V1V3: 拿来，跑去，走来，寄去，送去，买来，带去，etc.
>
> C. V1V2V3: 拿回来，送过去，带进去，走出来，买过来，etc.

If the verb takes an object, there are two possible structures.

> D. V1 + O + V3: 打电话来，带照相机去，寄一封信去，带行李来
>
> E. V1 + V3 + O: 打来电话，带来一位向导，买来吃的东西，
> 送去一本词典

II. 要是 ... 就 (if ... then): 要是 may either precede or follow a subject while 就 always occurs before a verb.

1. yaoshi + Subj1 + Predicate1 + Subj2 + jiu + Predicate2
    要是   你   每天都锻炼， 你的身体 就   会很健康。
    (If you exercise everyday, you will be very healthy.)

2. Subj1 + yaoshi + Predicate1 + Subj2 + jiu + Predicate2
    他   要是   不来，   我们   就   去找他。
    (If he does not come, we will go to see him.)

III. Contrast between 才 and 就: A sentence with 才 expresses an event which does not live up to one's expectation, therefore 才 never cooccur with Asp -了. A sentence with 就, on the contrary, indicates events exceeding one's expectation.

> 他八点才来。   (He didn't come until eight o'clock.)
>
> 他八点就来了。   (He came as early as eight o'clock.)

Practical Chinese Reader #41 Exercise A

I. Fill in blanks with appropriate vocabulary.

1. 昨天我们去长城玩，小张 ___ 我们带来了一位向导．

2. 那个亭子高高地站在山上，___ 人一样．

3. 每天上午到学院的车都很 ___，车上的人多 ___ 了，很多人都没有座位．

4. 我八点从家里 ___ 来，在路上 ___ 了半个小时才到这儿．

5. 我哥哥研究中国历史，他 ___ 中国很了解．

6. 天安门是一个高高的 ___ ___，前边有一个 ___ ___．

7. 我听 ___ 《李自成》是一本有名的 ___ ___，说的是崇祯 ___ ___ 在景山山 ___ 下吊死的故事．

8. 我们在门口等了一 ___ ___，他就进来了．

9. A: ___ ___ ___，我来晚了．

   B: ___ ___ ___，我们也刚到．

II. Fill in blanks with directional complements 来 or 去．

1. 向导和我们都在车上，你快上 ___ 吧．

2. 照相机在楼下．你下 ___ 拿吧．

3. 我哥哥从中国寄 ___ 了一本中文小说．

4. 我们在门口等你，你别在房间里说话，快出 ___ 吧．

5. 你看！我们给你带 ___ 了一些点心．

6. A: 天气真好，我们出 ___ 走走，好吗?

   B: 好啊，可是下午我有事儿，不能回 ___ 得太晚．

7. 我妹妹在法国，我给她寄 ___ 了五十元．

8. 他们到公园去玩的时候没带照相机 ___．

9. 王主任和我们在里边等你，请进 ___ 吧．

63

I. Fill in blanks with 才 or 就.

    1. 我们在外边等了很久 ___ 进来.

    2. 我们在外边等了一会儿 ___ 进来了.

    3. 今天车真挤，我们在路上花了一个小时 ___ 到这儿.

    4. 车 ___ 要开了，请大家上车吧.

    5. 我很早 ___ 听说过李自成的故事.

    6. 《李自成》这本小说我以前没听说过，到今天 ___ 知道有这本书.

    7. 要是我没带照相机，我 ___ 不能照相了.

    8. 你们先进教室去，我一会儿 ___ 来.

    9. 电影八点 ___ 开始，可是他们六点半 ___ 到电影院门口了.

    10. 你们从东边下山去．他们 ___ 在山脚下.

    11. 要是今天不考试，我 ___ 晚一点再去学院.

    12. 秋天了．树叶 ___ 要红了.

II. Insert 了 at appropriate positions in the following sentences.

    1. 我的同学给我送来两张运动会的票.

    2. 你带那本小说来吗?

    3. 学生不在这儿．他们进教室去.

    4. 他们去北海玩，带照相机去吗?

    5. 我给我姐姐寄一本小说去.

Complete the following dialogues:

1. A：对不起，＿＿＿＿＿＿＿＿＿＿＿＿＿＿＿．

   B：没关系，＿＿＿＿＿＿＿＿＿＿＿＿＿＿＿．

2. A：你怎么现在才来？

   B：＿＿＿＿＿＿＿＿＿＿＿＿＿＿＿＿＿．

3. A：＿＿＿＿＿＿＿＿＿＿＿＿＿＿＿＿＿．

   B：我没带来．　我明天给你送去．

4. A：＿＿＿＿＿＿＿＿＿＿＿＿＿＿＿＿＿．

   B：我们们从西边上山吧．

5. A：我不送了，请慢慢儿走．

   B：谢谢，＿＿＿＿＿＿＿＿＿＿＿＿＿＿＿．

6. A：＿＿＿＿＿＿＿＿＿＿＿＿＿＿＿＿＿．

   B：太好了，你想得真周到．

7. A：＿＿＿＿＿＿＿＿＿＿＿＿＿＿＿＿＿．

   B：要是明天不下雨，我们就去参观天安门广场．

8. A：今天外边人多极了．

   B：＿＿＿＿＿＿＿＿＿＿＿＿＿＿＿＿＿．

9. A：星期天你想作什么？

   B：＿＿＿＿＿＿＿＿＿＿＿＿＿＿＿ 或者 ＿＿＿＿＿＿＿＿＿＿＿＿＿＿．

Practical Chinese Reader #41 Exercise D

Translate into Chinese:

1. The guide is waiting for us at the entrance. Let's go out.

2. The building is in the square. Let's go over there to take a look.

3. Where are the guests? They went downstairs.

4. When will the driver return? We will go up the mountain in a while.

5. Having finished washing the clothes, he came back to the dormitory.

6. Have you brought your camera? Come over and take a picture of the pavilion.

7. I heard that he mailed twenty dollars to his younger brother.

8. I brought some snacks for you guys.

9. The doctor did not come to the infirmary.

10. We will go back home as soon as the semester ends.

Translate into Chinese:

1. If the weather is nice, you can see streets and buildings of Beijing clearly.

2. If I had received my friend's telephone call, I would not have gone out.

3. I didn't know anything about the story of this Chinese emperor until I read this historical novel.

4. The driver did not come back until when we were about to set off.

5. He heard that this novel was in the store. He then went downtown to buy it.

6. A: How come you came so late?
   B: I am sorry. The bus was too crowded. It took me more than an hour to get here.
   A: Have you brought the novel that I wanted?
   B: I left it at home. Either I can send it to you tomorrow or you can pick it up at my home (go to my home to take it) today.
   A: You're very thoughtful, but I'm going back home shortly.

Resultative verbs may be used in two different modes: the actual mode and the potential mode. What we have learned previously are those in actual mode, i.e., they denotes completed or expected to be completed events. The potential mode of the resultative verbs indicates whether a subject is able to cause the result to take place after taking the action.

The potential mode is expressed in the following forms.

  A. Positive: V1 + 得 + V2
          听得懂 (be able to listen and understand)
          看得见 (be able to see)
          收得到 (be able to receive)

  B. Negative: V1 + bu + V2
          看不完 (be unable to finish reading)
          修不好 (be unable to repair)
          找不到 (be unable to find)

  C. Interrogative: V1 得 V2 + V1 不 V2
          作得完作不完 (be able to finish?)
          看得懂看不懂 (be able to read and understand?)

There are certain verbs which belong to V2 category and which occur in a potential mode only.

  D. 了 -- to be able to
          完成得了 (be able to finish)
          用不了 (be unable to use up)
          回答不了 (be unable to answer)
          实现得了 (be able to carry out)

  E. 下 -- to accommodate
          放得下 (be able to store)
          挂得下 (have the space to hang)
          坐得下 (be able to seat)

  F. 动 -- to move
          跑得动 (have the energy to run)
          骑不动 (be unable to ride)
          跳不动 (be unable to jump)

Verbs with directional complements may also take potential mode.

  G. 上得去 (be able to go up)
      进不来 (be unable to come in)

Fill in blanks with resultative verb complements.

1. 你说得太快，我听不 ____.

2. 汽车挤得 ____ 八个人吗？

3. 那个书店里买得 ____ 《李自成》吗？

4. 这些活儿，那个退休的老工人干得 ____ 干不 ____?

5. 这个城太小了，看不 ____ 中国电影.

6. 你吃得 ____ 这么多东西吗？

7. 天气预报说，明天会下雨，我们去得 ____ 去不 ____ 公园？

8. 这张椅子太重，你搬*不 ____ 吧.

9. 我的裙子在哪儿？我不知道. 我找不 ____.

10. 这个广场停得 ____ 多少车？

11. 东西这么多，你拿得 ____ 拿不 ____?

12. 自行车太旧了，我想我修不 ____.

13. 箱子这么小，放得 ____ 这么多的东西吗？

14. 他身体不好，明天参加不 ____ 运动会了.

15. 衣服太多了，我洗不 ____.

16. 天安门广场站得 ____ 一百万人.

17. 这些工作你完成得 ____ 完成不 ____?

18. 我还看不 ____ 中文杂志.

19. 练习很多，你作得 ____ 吗？

20. 你写的字太小了，我看不 ____.

I. Fill in blanks with appropriate potential resultative verbs.

1. 山上的亭子你 _____ 吗？　　太远了，我 _____.

2. 这本小说你 _____ 吗？　　我的英文不好，我 _____.

3. 这些生词你 _____?　　生词不多，我 _____.

4. 今天老师给的练习你 _____ _____?

　　　　练习太难了，我 _____.

5. 在美国你们 _____ 中国菜吗？

　　　　美国有很多中国饭馆，我们 _____ 中国菜.

6. 今天照的照片你 _____ _____?

　　　　照片不太多，我想我 _____.

7. 那个正在修建的礼堂，明年 _____ 吗？

　　　　工人很多，我想 _____.

8. 箱子这么重，你 _____ 吗？

　　　　这个箱子不太重，我 _____.

9. 这辆自行车你 _____ 吗？

　　　　没问题，我一定 _____.

10. 桌子这么大，你 _____ 吗？

　　　　我一个人 _____.

11. 这间房间 _____ 四个人吗？

　　　　房间太小，_____ 四个人.

12. 这些活儿，你一个人 _____ _____?

　　　　活儿太重了，我一个人 _____.

II. Fill in blanks with proper words of measurement.

    1. 这个尺有多 ____?   一米.

    2. 这个房间有多 ____?   二十平方米*.

    3. 这张桌子有多 ____?   三十公斤*.

    4. 这位老爷爷今年多 ____ 岁数了?   他今年六十九岁.

    5. 这个门有多 ____ ?   三米.

    6. 这块布有多 ____ ?   一尺.

III. Write out the figures in Chinese characters.

    1.   6,428   _____

    2.   9,730   _____

    3.   5,200   _____

    4.   20,000   _____

    5.   45,000   _____

    6.   91,326   _____

Answer the following questions:

1. 天安门有多高?

2. 天安门广场站得下多少人?

3. 广场中间是什么? 西边是什么? 东边有什么?

4. 人民大会堂里边的大礼堂有多大? 一共几层?

5. 人民大会堂是哪年修建的? 用了多长时间完成的?

6. 人民大会堂坐得下多少人?

7. 人民大会堂是现代建筑还是古代建筑?

8. 典型的中国古代建筑有些什么?

9. 你们学院有多少学生?

10. 美国有多少人口(population)?

Translate into Chinese:

1. The film can't be developed by evening.

2. Can you see the pavilion on the hill?

3. I was unable to find the construction site you mentioned.

4. This car can seat five people.

5. The worker was unable to do such a heavy job.

6. There are so many things. Are you able to take them?

7. A: How tall is your younger brother?
   B: He is one hundred and senventy-nine centimeters tall.

8. A: How big is this auditorium?
   B: This auditorium is forty meters wide, and fifty meters long. It can accommodate several thousand people.

9. Although he is eighty years old, he can still walk around, hear things, and see things clearly.

10. A: How come you did not go into the auditorium?
    B: There were many people in the doorway. I could not get in.

I. More about verbs and their directional complements!

Verbal phrases which have the form V1V2V3 (see #41 Grammar Notes) may take a noun phrase as object or a place word as destination.

A. Place words as destinations

Subj (+ OE) + V1 + V2 + Place + V3 + OE
他　　　　　跑　上　楼　　去　了。
(He went upstairs.)

汽车　不能　　开　进　公园里　来。
(Cars are not allowed to drive into the park.)

B. When the verb of a sentence takes a direct object, there are two possibilities.

1. Subj (+ OE) + V1 + V2 + V3 + Object (+ OE)
他　给你　带　回　来　那本小说　了。
(He has brought back that novel for you.)

2. Subj (+ OE) + V1 + V2 + Object + V3
他　每星期　寄　回　一封信　去。
(He sends a letter back every week.)

II. The coordinator 又 ... 又
                    (both ... and; not only ... but also)

又 ... 又 is used to connect two verbal phrases. It must connect two expressions of the same nature, i.e., they must belong to the same grammatical category.

Subj + you + SV1/VP1 + you + SV2/VP2
他心里　又　高兴　　又　难过。
(He feels both happy and sad.)

今天　　又　刮风　　又　下雨。
(Not only is it windy, but it is also raining.)

74

Fill in blanks with appropriate vocabulary.

1. A：我 ____ 累 ____ 饿，我们找一 ____ 饭馆吃饭吧.

   B：我也有 ____ ____ 饿了.

2. 你看，穿 ____ 马路，那儿有一 ____ 小吃店，我们过去看看吧!

3. 这是一家北京 ____ ____ 的小吃店，里边坐着很多 ____ ____.

4. 小吃店里有 ____ 种小吃，都是北京风味的.

5. A：你们二位吃 ____ 什么?

   B：____ 四个油饼，两 ____ 炸糕.

6. 要是不 ____，再来一碗豌豆粥，____ ____ ____?

7. 别 ____ 中国菜我也吃过，可是我比 ____ 喜欢吃北京风味的中
   国菜.

8. 英国人喝茶跟中国人不一样，他们喜欢加 ____ ____ 和 ____.

9. 这家饭馆的服务员都很 ____ ____，服务也很 ____ ____. 我们
   走的时候，他们还请我们 ____ 意见.

10. 这是杏仁豆腐，你 ____ ____，作得好不好?

11. 你 ____ ____ 饿了吗? 怎么不多吃一点?

Fill in blanks with complex directional complements:

1. 礼堂门口怎么站着这么多的人？ 我们走 _____ 看看吧！

2. 一个孩子从屋里跑 _____，大声叫道："爸爸，你回来了."

3. "那幅画，挂在墙上了吗？"

   "已经挂 _____ 了."

4. 别站着说话，大家坐 _____ 谈吧！

5. 那张桌子，你从外边搬 _____ 了吗？

6. 他从箱子里拿 ____ 两件衬衫 ____.

7. 主席从门口走 ____ 礼堂 ____ 的时候，我们都站了 _____.

8. 我请弟弟从邮局买 _____ 二十张邮票.

9. 那个牌子已经从门上拿 _____ 了.

10.（在饭馆里）"菜太多了，吃不完."

   "没关系，吃不完我们可以带 _____."

11. 前边是绿灯*，我们可以快一点开 _____.

12. 我们都不在屋里，你快走 _____ 吧！

13. 我昨天没从老师那儿拿 ____ 本子 ____.

14. 写好的信你寄 _____了没有？

15. 我们今天可以去看京剧了. 小张昨天给我们送 _____ 两张票.

Translate into Chinese:

1. Who has walked in (here) from outside?

2. He did not run out (there).

3. The customer has walked into the restaurant.

4. The athlete swam across the river (to us).

5. Did you buy and bring some snacks back from the snack shop?

6. What did you bring back from school?

7. He did not take the camera back (here).

8. As for the letter, I've sent it out already.

9. The chef (master worker) brought out two fried cakes.

10. A: I feel both hungry and tired.
    B: Don't stand there. Sit down.

Translate into Chinese:

1. He took out two shirts from the suitcase.

2. Cars are not allowed to drive into the park.

3. A: I'm a bit hungry. Let's go into the snack shop to have
       something.
    B: O.K.
    C: What would you like to eat?
    B: Is there a menu*?
    C: Yes. Here it is.
    A: This restaurant has all kinds of Beijing style snacks.
    B: Give us two deep-fried pancakes and two bowls of almond
       junket.
    C: Anything else?
    A: No. Your service is superb.
    C: It's our duty.

Write a short script describing a scene in a Chinese restaurant.

Suggested vocabulary: 服务员，顾客，菜单*，饿，渴*，汽水，好吃，

别的，风味.

I. 是 ... 的 as a focus marker

是 may be placed before an element with 的 usually occurring
at the end of a sentence to express that the element is the
focus of the sentence where it occurs.   The element can be a
subject, a place word, a time expression, a prepositional
phrase indicating manner, or a verb phrase.   The construction
is used with the presupposition that an event has taken place
and the speaker intends to know or to give more information
about it.

A.   Subj + 是 + Time + Predicate + 的

    X. 我母亲   到中国去了。
        (My mother went to China.)

    Y. 她   是   什么时候 去   的?
        (WHEN did she go?)

    X. 她   是   上星期   去   的。
        (She went last week.)

B.   他是从上海来的。
          (It was from Shanghai that he came.)

          我们是坐飞机去的。
          (It was by air that we went.)

          他们不是来工作的。
          (They did not come to work.)

          是张老师给我们介绍颐和园的。
          (It was Prof. Zhang who told us about the Summer
           Palace.)

Note: When a verb takes an object, 的 may occur either inbetween
      the verb and its object or at the end of a sentence. For
      example:

      他是什么时候去的广州?

      他是什么时候去广州的?

80

II. Sentences with subject-verb reversion are those where expressions of location are more emphasized.

Location + VP + NP
他家   来了   几位客人。
(There were several guests at his house.)

从车里   走下来   几个人。
(There came several people from the car.)

III. Exclamatory sentences are expressed by 多(么) ... 啊，or by 太 ... 了。

Subj   + duo(mo)/tai + SV + Particle
那位服务员   多   热情   啊!
(How nice that clerk is!)

这儿的风景   多么   美   啊!
(How beautiful the scenery is!)

太   好   了!
(That is terrific!)

IV. 只有 ... 才 (only when ... then) connects two sentences.
Both 只有 and 才 are placed before a verb if the subjects of the sentences in question are identical.   只有 occurs at the beginning of the first sentence if the two subjects have different referents.

A. Subj + zhiyou + Predicate1 (+ Subj) + cai + Predicate2
你   只有   自己去看看，(你)   才 能了解那儿的情况。
(Only when you take a look yourself can you understand the condition there.)

B. zhiyou + Subj1 + Predicate1 + Subj2 + cai + Predicate2
只有   他   来，   我们   才   能去。
(Only when he comes can we go.)

V. SV + 得 + VP (so SV that ... VP)

他难过得哭了起来。
(He was so sad that he started to cry.)

她累得不能走路。
(She was so tired that she could not walk at all.)

81

Fill in blanks with appropriate vocabulary.

1. 秋天来了，叶子都红了． 外边的 ＿＿＿＿ ＿＿＿＿ 很美，像一 ＿＿＿＿
   画儿一样．

2. 春天的时候，地上的绿 ＿＿＿＿ 都长出来了．

3. ＿＿＿＿ 山是一种很好的运动．

4. ＿＿＿＿ ＿＿＿＿ 每天从东边出来，从西边下去．

5. 这几年中国和美国的 ＿＿＿＿ ＿＿＿＿ 很多．

6. 昆明湖后边是一 ＿＿＿＿ 山，叫万寿山．

7. 我们的中文一天 ＿＿＿＿ 一天进步．

8. A：明天你们去颐和园玩，我作你们的向导．

   B：太好 ＿＿＿＿！

9. 你看！这儿的风景多么美 ＿＿＿＿！

10. 明年夏天我决定到中国去 ＿＿＿＿ 行．

11. A：你常常出去看电影吗？

    B：不，只有星期六晚上我 ＿＿＿＿ 出去看电影．

12. 他们不 ＿＿＿＿ 来度假*的，他们 ＿＿＿＿ 来谈贸易的．

13. 他听了以后高兴得跳 ＿＿＿＿ ＿＿＿＿．

14. 颐和园是有名的古典 ＿＿＿＿ ＿＿＿＿．

15. 冬天来了．天气一天比 ＿＿＿＿ ＿＿＿＿ 冷了．

Following sentences are possible answers to certain questions.
Give an appropriate quertion form to each of them.

1. 我是上星期去的颐和园.

2. 我弟弟是一九七五年生的.

3. 他们是坐飞机从广州到北京的.

4. 他是跟两个同学一起到昆明旅行的.

5. 他们这次是来参观工厂的.

6. 我不是从公园去的. 我是从饭馆去的.

7. 草地上坐着几个年轻人.

8. 你只有自己去看看，才能了解到那儿的情况.

9. 我不是骑车来的.

10. 湖边有一个亭子.

Answer questions on the basis of the text:

1. 颐和园是哪一年开始修建的?

2. 万寿山为什么叫这个名字?

3. 万寿山上有什么?

4. 颐和园里的长廊有多长?

5. 长廊上边有什么?

6. 哪儿有一个白塔?

7. 古波说的山上的画儿是什么?

8. 你看过《三国演义》吗? 那是一本什么样的小说?

9. 昆明湖在哪儿?

Practical Chinese Reader #44 Exercise D

Translate into Chinese:

1. It was last week that her mother came.

2. It was with a tourist group that they traveled.

3. When was it that he decided to come with the trade
   delegation?

4. It was by boat that they went to Japan.

5. The car came from behind.

6. From the lakeside, an old man walked toward us here.

7. From the car, several people walked out.

8. How cordial the sales clerk is!

9. How beautiful the scenery here is!

Translate into Chinese:

1. Nobody knows how much he likes Chinese paintings.

2. Only when the sun is out is Kunming Lake as bright as a mirror.

3. Only when you speak more, listen more, and read more can you learn a foreign language well.

4. Only when you walk to the lakeside can you see the bridge.

5. He was so sad that he began to cry.

6. She was so happy that she shouted loudly: "That's great!"

7. I feel that Chinese is becoming more interesting everyday.

8. The quality of this type of chinaware has been improved year by year.

Fill in blanks with 的，地 or 得.

1. 熊猫吃 ____ 是竹叶． 他们在竹林里不停 ____ 走来走去．

2. 观众看见了可爱 ____ 熊猫都热烈 ____ 鼓掌．

3. 从山上 ____ 公园看过去，山下 ____ 建筑看 ____ 清清楚楚．

4. 见到了从国外回来 ____ 朋友，他高兴 ____ 跳了起来．

5. 这儿 ____ 风景真美！ 青 ____ 山，绿 ____ 水，远远 ____ 山

   上还有一个亭子．

6. 每个学生都认真 ____ 在图书馆里学习．

7. 孩子们高高兴兴 ____ 到学校去了．

8. 她女儿有一双大大 ____ 眼睛，非常像她妈妈．

9. 今天照 ____ 照片洗 ____ 好吗？

10. 他们不是来工作 ____，他们是来旅行 ____．

11. 熊猫 ____ 样子又可爱又可笑． 肥肥 ____ 身体，短短 ____

    腿，眼睛上像戴着墨镜．

12. 雪下 ____ 这么大，我们出 ____ 去吗？

Fill in blanks with 才 or 就.

1. 车 ____ 要开了，请大家坐好.

2. ____ 他一个人来，别人都出去玩儿了.

3. 只有作完功课以后，我们 ____ 能出去看电影.

4. 我 ____ 有一件绿衬衫.

5. 我找了半个多小时 ____ 找到你家.

6. 他昨天跳舞跳得太晚了. 今天上午十点钟 ____ 起床.

7. 他三岁的时候 ____ 跟母亲到外国去了.

8. 要是明天是晴天，我们 ____ 到颐和园去玩儿.

9. 昨天上午我们没回宿舍，到晚上吃完了饭以后我们 ____ 回去.

10. 昨天吃了晚饭以后，我们 ____ 去听音乐了.

11. 你从这儿往西走，过两个路口，____ 可以看见那个小吃店了.

12. 我们又累又饿，在小吃店里吃了四个油饼，六块炸糕，两碗豆

腐汤 ____ 回家.

Give negative forms for the following sentences:

1. 他说汉语说得很流利.

2. 这个工厂的工人工作得跟那个工厂的工人一样认真.

3. 我昨天从箱子里找出一条裙子来.

4. 在那个书店里买得到这本英文小说.

5. 我在动物园看过两次熊猫.

6. 熊猫的样子比别的动物可爱.

7. 他们是跟贸易团到广州来的.

8. 从非洲来的学生跟从南亚来的一样多.

9. 那个礼堂坐得下五千人.

10. 我们作完了练习才去看电影.

11. 那张桌子两个人搬得动.

Translate into Chinese:

1. A: Did you hear what the chairman said?
   B: No, the platform is too far away. I was unable to hear clearly.

2. There were so many people in the zoo. We could not get in.

3. A: How big is the table?
   B: It's five feet long, three feet wide.

4. The look of a panda is both lovely and funny.

5. As soon as she saw her daughter, she was so excited that she began to cry.

6. I've brought a tour guide for you.

7. If your sister does not come and take the camera, we will then mail it to her.

8. That novel was written ten years ago. He has not written any book since then.

把-Construction

A sentence with Ba-construction emphasizes how an object of a sentence is disposed or handled. In a 把-sentence the object of a verb is preposed to the position before the verb and after 把 to form a prepositional phrase. For example:

Subject (+Adv/Neg) + Ba + Object + Verb + Aspect/Complement

他　　　　　　　　把　衣服　　洗　　　　干净了。
(He washed the clothes.)
你　　　　　　　　把　录音机　带　　　　来了　　吗?
(Did you bring the tape-recorder?)
(请)你　　　　　　把　窗户　　开　　　　开。
(Please open the window.)
我　　　　　　　　把　这件事儿 忘　　　　了。
(I forgot this matter.)
你　　　　　　　　把　名字　　写　　　　一写。
(Write your name.)
他　　没　　　　　把　信　　　写　　　　得很好。
(He did not write the letter well.)
我　　明天　　　　把　照相机　带　　　　来。
(I will bring the camera tomorrow.)
向导　　　　　　　把　那个学生 带　　　　来了。
(The guide has brougnt the student here.)

There are several noticeable features about a Ba-sentence:

1. The verb must be an action verb. Verbs such as 喜欢，有，是，知道，etc. can not occur in a Ba-structure.

2. The object must be a definite noun, i.e., it must have a referent.

3. The verb connot stand alone, i.e., the verb must be followed by other element(s). The element(s) may simply be an aspect marker 了 or 着, or a directional complemnent, a quantitative verb modifier, a degree adverbial, or a resultative complement.

4. Negation 不/没有 is placed before the preposition 把. Other expressions such as time expressions or modals also occur before the preposition.

Fill in blanks with appropriate vocabulary.

I.　　　　帕兰卡昨天晚上睡觉的时候没把窗户 ____ 上，今天可能感 ____
了。她觉得很不 ____ ____ ，头 ____ ，咳 ____ ，又发 ____ ，病
得很厉 ____ 。

　　　　她到 ____ ____ 去看大夫。大夫给她 ____ 了体温，说是重感
冒，要 ____ 院。听了大夫的话，她 ____ ____ 办住院手续，在病
房里躺了一天，____ 了药，____ 了针以后，已经 ____ 多了。

II.　1.　请把门开 ____ 。

　　2.　我已经把电视关 ____ 了。

　　3.　你把我带来的录音听一 ____ 吧。

　　4.　你把饺子包 ____ 了吗?

　　5.　请他把带去的东西检查 ____ ____ 。

　　6.　请护士* 把病人的体温量一 ____ 。

　　7.　你把花儿都种 ____ 了没有?

　　8.　妈妈把衣服都洗 ____ 了。

　　9.　你把药吃 ____ 没有?

　　10.　他没把我的照相机带 ____ 。

Change the following sentences into sentences with 把-construction.

1. 请你立刻开开录音机，我想听听。

2. 昨天晚上我没关上窗户，所以感冒了。

3. 这件事儿，他们告诉了我。

4. 大夫请护士* 量一量他的体温。

5. 姥姥包好了饺子，大家就开始吃了。

6. 录音机录上了他说的话。

7. 他忘了吃药了，所以病没好。

8. 那张照片你还给了他没有？

9. 请拿出挂号证* 来。

10. 葡萄他没洗干净。

Answer questions with 把-construction.

1. 我的录音机怎么不见了?

2. 他送来的葡萄在哪儿?

3. 病房里为什么这么冷?

4. 电视机还开着吗?

5. 你给你朋友寄去了什么?

6. 大夫对你作了些什么?

7. 我的衣服在哪儿?

8. 我要带走的东西怎么了?

9. 我们什么时候可以吃饺子?

I. Translate into Chinese:

Doctor: What's wrong with you?

Patient: I have a headache, and a cough too. It's very likely
         that I have a cold.

Doctor: Let me take your temperature. Open your mouth.

Patient: Do I have a fever?

Doctor: Yes, but not too serious. How long have you had the
          discomfort?

Patient: Last evening.

Doctor: You have a cold. You will feel better after taking
          some medicine. here's the prescription.

Patient: How should I take the medicine?

Doctor: Four times a day, two tablets each time.

Patient: Thank you.

II. Controlled composition.

    Write a paragraph in Chinese about your experience of seeing a
    doctor. You thought you caught a cold and explained to your
    doctor what happened. The doctor did the routine check-up on
    you. You did not get better after having taken the medicine
    prescribed by the doctor. However, you finally got better
    because of some other measures.

    (You finish the story.)

I.   把-construction

把-construction must be employed in cases where resultative verbs or verbs with post-verbal prepositions take definite nouns as their objects.

A.   Verbs with post-verbal prepositional phrases

在 -- at, in, on
他把笔忘在家里了。   (He left his pen at home.)
你把书放在哪儿了?   (Where did you put the book?)

到 -- to
我把椅子拿到楼上去了。   (I took the chair upstairs.)
他们把我送到车站。   (They saw me to the station.)

给 -- to
我把钱交给了售票员。
(I gave the money to the ticket seller.)
请把书留给他。
(Please leave the book to him.)

B.   Verbs with resultative complements

成 -- into; for
他想把房子修建成那个样子。
(He intends to build the house like that.)
我把他看成了中国人。
(I took him for a Chinese.)

作 -- as
他们把他看作家里人。
(They consider him as a family member.)
上海人把 "喝茶" 叫作 "吃茶"。
(People in Shanghai refer to "喝茶" as "吃茶".)

II.   除了 ... (以外) ... 还 (in addition to)
        除了 ... (以外) ... 都 (except)

A.   昨天下午除了游泳,他还钩鱼了。
     (Yesterday afternoon he fished in addition to swimming.)

B.   除了他骑自行车去以外,我们都坐车去了。
     (We all went by car but he rode a bicycle.)

96

Fill in blanks with suitable vocabulary:

1. 鲁迅的故居的院子里有两 ____ 枣树.

2. 这 ____ 房子有三 ____ 卧室.

3. 我看过一 ____ 鲁迅写的文章，也看过他写的一 ____ 小说.

4. 美国诗人 Emily Dickinson 的 ____ ____ 在麻州安城.

5. 去年我到中国去了． 回来以后，我很 ____ ____ 在中国的生活.

6. 参观了有名的人的故居以后，很多人把 ____ ____ 写在留言簿上.

7. 除了他们俩 ____ ____，别的人 ____ 喜欢爬山.

8. 房子的北边 ____ 着另一个房子.

9. 这句话我看不懂，请你给我 ____ ____ 一下.

10. ____ ____ 历史以外，我 ____ 喜欢艺术.

11. 鲁迅给中国人民留下了 ____ ____ 的文化遗产.

Fill in blanks with 成，作，在，到，or 给.

1. 北京人把 ice-lolly 叫 ____ 冰棍儿.

2. 老师把这个伟大的文学家的生活介绍 ____ 我们.

3. 我们把两株树种 ____ 院子里.

4. 对不起，我忘了把书带 ____ 学校里来，我把书留 ____ 家里了.

5. 我把他给我的照片留 ____ 纪念*.

6. 父母都想把孩子培养 ____ 好青年.

7. 请把句子翻译 ____ 中文.

8. 大家把他选 ____ 主席.

9. 他们把车开 ____ 飞机场去接他.

10. 我已经把练习交 ____ 老师了.

11. 这个设计师 (designer) 把礼堂设计 ____ 现在这个样子.

12. 请你把这件行李带 ____ 我哥哥请他寄 ____ 中国去.

13. 那个老人把这个年轻人看 ____ 自己的儿子.

14. 他父亲的遗产都留 ____ 了他.

15. 他把 '大夫' 念 ____ 了 'dafu'.

Make sentences:

1. 把 ... 看作

2. 把 ... 作成

3. 把 ... 留给

4. 把 ... 拿到

5. 把 ... 叫作

6. 除了 ... 以外 ... 也

7. 除了 ... 以外 ... 都

8. 除了 ... 以外 ... 还

Translate into Chinese:

1. They wrote their names in the visitor's book.

2. I have already returned the book to the library.

3. They spent ten years developing the small clinic into a hospital.

4. They did not say "good-bye" to me until they saw me off at the station.

5. My classmates asked me to bring the tape-recorder to you.

6. They elected this worker to be director of the factory.

7. Everyone got the flu except him.

8. Besides this article, what other writings of Lu Xun's have you read?

9. The weather here is pretty good except (the fact that) it is a bit cold in winter.

10. The guide led the visitors to the courtyard.

Interrogative pronouns (IP) which have general denotations

A.   As subjects

    IP   +   都/也   (+ Neg) + Predicate
    谁   都   不   想睡觉。
    (Nobody would like to sleep.)

    什么   都   好。
    (Anything is good.)

    哪儿   都   有人。
    (There are people everywhere.)

B.   As objects

    Subject + IP   +   都/也 (+ Neg)   +   Predicate
    他   什么   都   想试一试。
    (He would like to try anything.)

    这位作家   哪个国家   都   去过。
    (This writer has been to every country.)

Fill in blanks with vocabulary:

1. 中国的春节就 ____ 圣诞节一样，是 ____ 家人团聚的 ____ ____.

2. 春节的时候见到别人要给人 ____ 年.

3. 在春节的时候，常常可以看到 "恭 ____ 新 ____" 这四个字.

4. 新年的时候，全家人在一起 ____ 年. 孩子们都 ____ 新衣服，新鞋，____ 新帽子，在外边 ____ 爆竹，____ 灯笼，高兴 ____ 了.

5. 中国新年是 ____*历正月 ____ ____.

6. 春节的前一晚叫作 ____ ____*.

7. 吃年夜饭*是中国人的 ____ ____.

8. 春节的时候，很多人在门上 ____ 春联，在墙上 ____ 年画儿.

9. 吃年夜饭的时候，桌上总是 ____ 着很多菜.

10. 我真 ____ 想 ____ 他写字写得这么整齐.

11. A: 您要的东西我都带来了.

    B: 谢谢您，真太 ____ ____ 您了.

12. 他家里总是 ____ 扫得很 ____ 净.

13. A: 他 ____ ____ ____ 没有回家?

    B: ____ ____ 最近比较忙，所以没有回家.

Complete the following sentences by supplying verbal phrases and make them sentences with a passive meaning.

1. 过年的饭菜

2. 这篇文章

3. 我买来的花儿

4. 客人的房间

5. 他带来的新年礼物

6. 桌上的东西

7. 你朋友要的春联

8. 孩子们的爆竹

9. 邮票都

Complete the following sentences with the given interrogative pronouns.

1. 全班除了这个学生以外，_____（谁）

2. 除了鱼以外，_____（什么菜）

3. 明天我全天都有空儿 _____（什么时候）

4. 我的车坏了，还没修好，所以 _____（哪儿）

5. 菜已经作好了，但是 _____（谁）

6. 练习太多了，_____（怎么）

7. 昨天我去百货大楼买东西，可是人太多了，所以 _____

_____（什么）

8. 你知道谁想要这件礼物？_____（谁）

9. 谁想去中国参观？_____（哪个作家）

10. 春节的时候哪儿可以看到年画儿？_____（哪儿）

Answer the following questions:

1. 春联最常贴在哪儿?

2. 春联都是用什么纸写的?

3. 在美国，新年的时候放爆竹吗?

4. 春节为什么要放爆竹?

5. 为什么中国人吃年夜饭的时候要吃鱼?

6. 今年圣诞节你和谁一起过的?

7. 今年新年你过得怎么样?

8. 你看过中国年画儿吗?

Translate into Chinese:

1. The room has not been cleaned up yet.

2. The lantern with the characters "Happy New Year" written on it has been hung up.

3. All the food for the New Year have been prepared.

4. Pandas are lovely animals. Everyone likes them.

5. I did not realize that he ate nothing but American food.

6. He will read books by any writer, since he loves reading.

7. I heard that people here eat dumplings at New Year, but you may have them any day.

8. We came late today because we went to bed a bit late last night.

9. I did not buy that lamp, because I did not bring enough money with me.

10. Since this winter is relatively mild, I spent my Christmas at home.

I. Sentences of passive voice

        Recipient + Neg + Prep + Actor + Verb + OE

        我的自行车   让   他   骑   走了。
        (My bicycle was ridden away by him.)

        我们   都   被   这个作品 感动   了。
        (We were all moved by this literary work.)

        我的纸   没   叫   风   刮   走。
        (My paper was not blown away by the wind.)

        照相机   被   他们   拿   走了吗?
        (Was the camera taken away by them?)

II. The connective 不但 ... 而且 connects either two predicates
    or two sentences. Its position of occurrence varies.

    A. Subject + 不但 + Predicate1 + 而且 + Predicate2
        这个话剧   不但   写得好,   而且   演得也很好。
        (This play was not only well written but well performed.)

    B. 不但 + Subj1 + Predicate1 + 而且 + Subj2 + Predicate2
        不但   中国人 怀念他   而且   外国人 也怀念他。
        (Not only did the Chinese miss him, but foreigners missed
        him too.)

III. 连 ... 也/都 (even) may apply to

    A. a subject

        连 + Subject + 都/也 + Predicate
        连   孩子们   都   被吸引住了。
        (Even the children were enchanted.)

        连   这位作家 也   来了。
        (Even this writer has come.)

    B. an object

        Subj + 连 + Obj + 都/也 + Predicate
        他   连   衣服   也   没有换。
        (He did not even change his clothes.)

        她   连   椅子 都   带来了。
        (She even brought the chair with her.)

Fill in blanks with appropriate vocabulary.

1. ____ ____ 是记一个人一天的事或者感想.

2. 这个话剧要在那个很大的 ____ ____ 演出.

3. 那个话剧的 ____ ____ 非常成功.

4. 作家，画家，演员*都是 ____ ____ 家.

5. 《茶馆》是老舍写的有名的 ____ ____ 之一.

6. 他的小说我以前看过，但是看他的话剧这 ____ 是第一次.

7. 请你给我正 ____ 的回答.

8. 中国的旧社会是一个黑 ____ 的社会.

9. 我们不但被这个话剧吸 ____ 住了，____ ____ 被它 ____ 动了.

10. 在旧社会，很多中国人民 ____ 抓，____ 杀. 有的还 ____ 逼
    得卖儿卖女.

11. 我 ____ ____ 喜欢听女高音*独唱*，而且喜欢听民乐*.

12. 那个 ____ 人作了很多 ____事 ，所以被抓了.

13. 他连衣服 ____ 没换就出去了.

Change into passive voice:

1. 这个剧感动了劳动人民.

2. 大家把老舍叫作 "人民艺术家".

3. 小张把我的照相机借走了.

4. 这个演员成功的演出把我们都吸引住了.

5. 这个作家还没把他的话剧翻译成法文.

6. 在那个时代，有人不但把爱国青年抓了，而且还杀了.

7. 他不但把我的自行车借走了，而且把我的汽车也开走了.

8. 坏人连孩子也杀了.

9. 风把报纸都刮走了.

10. 除了小王以外，我谁都请了.

Change the sentences into 连...也 construction with the under-
lined phrases as the focus of the structures. For example:

我没有喝茶就走了.
我连茶也没有喝就走了.

1. 那个坏人被这个话剧感动了.

2. 那个坏作品让人借走了.

3. 我把我爸爸给我的十元钱化了.

4. 没有钱的人不但没有吃的，穿的，而且被逼得把儿女卖了.

5. 他没吃完饭就走了.

Complete the following sentences:

1. 不但中国人过年的时候要团聚，而且 _____.

2. 这儿的冬天不但雪下得很多，而且 _____.

3. 我不但把功课作完了，而且连 _____.

4. 那个音乐会不但有合唱*，独唱*，而且 _____.

5. 他不常看话剧，连 _____.

Translate into Chinese:

1. Lao She was one of the most famous writers in China.

2. What this writer wrote about was conditions in the Old Society.

3. The synopsis of this play has yet been translated into English.

4. The audience was enchanted by the language of the play.

5. Not only were the patriots arrested and killed, but the poor were forced to work.

6. This novel not only enhanced my knowledge of the Chinese history but also deepened my understanding of the Chinese people.

7. We not only read his works but also translated them into other languages.

8. Even the actor was moved by his own successful performance.

9. The delegation stayed in Beijing for a short time. They did not even visit Yi-He-Yuan (the Summer Palace).

10. Not only have the students not been to a tea house, but not even their teacher has been to one.

Fill in blanks with appropriate vocabulary.

1. 这位有名的作家的作品，有的我看过，____ ____ 我没看过.

2. 今年我是在中国过 ____ 春节.

3. 这家饭馆的小吃，____ 好吃又便宜.

4. ____ ____ 外边天气太冷了，所以我们昨晚没出去.

5. ____ ____ 这位伟大的艺术家逝世了，但是大家还是怀念着他.

6. 青年们都 ____ 鲁迅看作自己的好朋友，好老师.

7. 我一看见她 ____ 觉得她像我的姐姐.

8. 你要是今天不太忙，____ 请到我家来坐坐.

9. 只有不太忙的时候我 ____ 能到外边走走.

10. 除了游泳 ____ ____，他们 ____ 钓鱼了.

11. 谁 ____ 大家叫作 "人民艺术家"?

12. 这位艺术家 ____ ____ 在中国很有名，而且在世界上也很有名.

13. 谁 ____ 会被这儿的风景吸引住.

14. ____ ____ 风雪很大，但是梅花还是挺立着.

15. 太热了，请你 ____ 窗户打开.

16. 我们都去参观那个画展了，连老师 ____ 去了.

17. 这个学生不很聪明，____ 不用功.

18. 他每天 ____ 到十二点就睡觉了.

19. ____ ____ 每天练习说汉语，汉语才能说得很流利.

20. ____ ____ 每天练习说汉语，汉语就能说得很流利.

Complete the following sentences:

1. 花儿被

2. 我把钱

3. 他们是上星期六

4. 礼堂里边

5. 因为我们认识的时间不长，

6. 我们一到公园

7. 除了小张以外，

8. 要是

9. 只有

10. 不但

11. 虽然

12. 观众都被这个剧吸引住了，连

Practical Chinese Reader #50 Exercise C

Translate into Chinese:

1. It was in 1976 that the premier passed away.

2. Only when one writes characters stroke by stroke can one write them beautifully.

3. Last Sunday was their twentieth wedding anniversary.

4. We read his diary page by page.

5. This painter was one of the greatest artists in the world.

6. The guide at the art gallery said with smile, "Your comments, please."

7. The one who attracted our attention most was a little girl of six or seven (years old).

8. The students came out from the auditorium one by one. The last one was a boy of thirteen (years old).